Pat

"GIVE THEM HOPE!"

Eph 3:18-20

Winning
The Battle For
Our Heavenly Hope

Laura K. Black

Laura Black RN, BSN

Printed in the USA by

MORRIS PUBLISHING

3212 East Highway 30 • Kearney, NE 68847 • 1-800-650-7888

DEDICATION

To all the sheep—that feel so beat,
And for those who wish to be
A Good Samaritan
To God's sheep.

Foreword

I was dying inside and did not know,
until my Lord revealed it, so,
I could see and face the pain;
allowing Jesus to heal me again!

Even after He exposes the wounds in me,
He applies His balm so effortlessly.
Sometimes He uses a well-spoken word.
Repeatedly, His voice I've heard,
Saying;
I can do above all you can think,
exceedingly, abundantly, in only a wink.
I'll be the resurrection and the life to you,
exalt you in time and make dreams come true.

You cannot get it by trusting in the arms of flesh,
you have only to believe my Word and rest!

My power is on you, in you, around you,
let me penetrate those walls that surround you.
I'll wipe away every tear,
and hold your heart so very near.
No more struggling, your faith I've seen,
now I'm here upon the scene,
to set you in a larger place,
to show you my amazing grace!

All this my child is so you will mend—
With All My Love,
Your
"Good Samaritan"

INTRODUCTION

Approximately seven years ago I cried unto the Lord with tears streaming down my face. I had to know—"What, God, is your will for my life?" Into my heart and spirit the answer came very clearly—

"Give Them Hope!"

I did not understand at that time what God meant. However, the Lord in His perfect timing and infinite faithfulness would teach me what it is to feel broken, hopeless, and neglected. Then He birthed through my season of personal anguish words that will minister to the hurting.

From that wilderness experience the Holy Spirit continued to teach me how to win the various battles targeted against my faith (hope). And through these 70 devotions it is my passionate desire to help others to build, restore, and regain their hope in God.

This collection of modern psalms share the struggle, the stress, and the strain in a very personal and transparent style. These meditations will show that God is in the midst of every experience and that He is always working things out for the good of His children.

I think that most will agree that in these times, good words are needed to strengthen our heavenly hope. *"Heaviness in the heart of man maketh it stoop: But a good word maketh it glad."* (Proverbs 12:25)

CONTENTS

Devotions

For

Winning
The Battle Against
Our Heavenly Hope
****

Psalms 119:114
"I hope in thy word"

UNDERNEATH HIS WINGS
(Battling the fear of rejection)

Jesus stood arrayed in light,
hugged my soul
and made me right!
He spoke a word
unto my heart
saying;

//
***"I Love you, and I accept you,
just as you are!"***
//

As He spoke all I could see
were huge feathery wings
encircling me!
It lasted a moment,
that was enough,
for His awesome, powerful,
unfailing love—
to penetrate the fear, the pain,
to reassure
that I belong to Him!

Tears of great joy rocked my soul—
forever changed because
I know,
The Sun of Righteousness
and His wings—
cover, heal,
and remain!

There is healing
(even from the fear of rejection)
in His wings.

Malachi 4:2
"But unto you that fear my name
shall the Sun of righteousness arise with
healing in his wings;..."

As a hen gathers and protects her offspring
so the Lord also shields and protects
those who trust in Him.

Psalms 91:4
"He will shield you with his wings.
He will shelter you with his feathers.
His faithful promises
are your armor and protection." 1

The greatest truth in my life has been a shield
against the voice of the enemy,
and that truth
is the same for everyone who accepts Christ—
that we are loved and accepted
just the way we are.

Psalms 36:7
"How excellent is thy lovingkindness,
O God!
therefore the children of men
put their trust
under
the shadow of thy wings."

DIDN'T YOU?
(Battling condemnation)

Didn't you deny the Lord three times in one night?
Didn't you break your vows to stand up and fight?
Didn't you declare, life or death that you'd be true?
Didn't you weep so bitterly, the unfaithful blues?

Didn't you betray the love of your life?
Oh, Peter! Who can make that right?
How could a sinful, fallen-failure like you,
ever expect to be used?

What a mental riot,
the thoughts of a coward like you;
to head the church,
who would listen to the likes of you?

Did you ever think
that you would cower down,
in the heat of the moment,
as they smacked your Lord around?

Didn't you pray when Jesus asked you to?
Didn't you discern His agony?
Didn't you?

And where were you—
when Jesus bled and died?
Aren't you
THE ROCK
that Jesus recognized?

It's Grace and Mercy,
that's why He picked you out;
He knew we could relate
to one
with so many
nagging
doubts!

It's Grace and Mercy,
that's why He called on you;
He knew we could identify
with one
who has failed too!

It's Grace and Mercy,
that's why
He prayed you through;
And
He knew we could empathize
with one
who needed His prayers too!

Our Heavenly Hope
****
His Prayers!

Luke 22:31-32
"And the Lord said, Simon, Simon,
behold,
Satan has desired to have you,
that he may sift you as wheat:
But I have prayed for thee,
that thy faith fail not:
and when thou art converted,
strengthen thy brethren."

ACHING HEART
(Battling a broken heart)

Too much aching in my soul—
Who really cares? Who really knows?
Too much aching in my heart,
so broken and falling apart.

Too much aching in my mind—
looking for something I just cannot find.
Too much aching for too many years,
I'm so tired of all these tears.

Too much aching I just cannot see—
Why You won't heal this ache in me.
What pleasure can my Lord obtain
to see me languishing in all this pain.

The problem my child is that you do not see
my handiwork of love in thee.
You're focused on what's hurting you now—
I'm more concerned that you would allow,
me to use your aching heart
for those so broken and falling apart.
You see pain is a gift—it can set you free
to share my love more compassionately!

Our Heavenly Hope
****

God sent His Word and restores us
according to our faith in His Words.

Psalm 119:28
"I weep with grief; encourage me by your word." 1

JUDGMENTAL EYES
(Battling self-righteousness)

Rejected, despised, brutally criticized,
are those that we see with our judgmental eyes.

A woman of sin, who's love was so much,
had the nerve, had the gall; The Master to touch.
The self-righteous drew near, they drew near to see,
how this prophet of God could grant her such liberty.

A filthy old beggar cried out to see,
despite all of those trying to get him to leave.
He cried; "Son of David: Have mercy on me."
He cried; "Son of David: I just want to see."

A passionate soul all alone in a tree, thinking:
Why would Jesus even look up at me, thinking;
Why would The Master even look up at me?
Then Jesus said; "Zacheus, come down from that tree."
"For this very night, I'll be dining with thee!"

Christ bled and died, so cruelly crucified,
while men looked down on Him
with their judgmental eyes.

Our Heavenly Hope
****
Pray that our eyes will be
focused on setting others free,
not on their sin, but on their recovery.

2 Corinthians 3:17
"...where the Spirit of the Lord is, there is freedom." [2]

SPIRITUAL BULLIES
(Battling bullies)

Spiritual bullies always come around,
trying to discourage and push me around.
But, I have a Savior, He listens when I call,
and when He stands up over them—
they cower and they fall!

Spiritual bullies—they're Satan's envoy,
sent to deter me, my vision to destroy.
But, I have a Savior, He listens when I call,
and they don't stand a chance—
because He's bigger than them all!

Our Heavenly Hope
****
The Word clearly tells us we will be attacked and
we will suffer, but our hope is that
the God of all grace will himself restore us.

1 Peter 5:7-10
"Cast all your anxieties on him
because he cares for you. Be self-controlled and alert.
Your enemy the devil prowls around like a roaring
lion looking for someone to devour.
Resist him, standing firm in the faith,
because you know that your brothers throughout the
world are undergoing the same kind of sufferings.
And the God of all grace, who called you
to his eternal glory in Christ,
after you have suffered for awhile,
will himself restore you
and make you strong, firm, and stedfast." [2]

"CRUCIFY HIM!"
(Battling envy)

They delivered Jesus out of envy, it's true,
not one fault could Pilate prove.
Even Pilate's wife said;
"Have nothing to do with this innocent man."
In a dream she was troubled
over and over again.

Pilate did not listen to this woman with sense,
He gave in to the crowds
and men of violence—
Saying;
"Crucify, Crucify, Crucify Him!"

The flesh wants to see
others humiliated/debased
Yet nothing we do will ever erase,
the agony Christ bore in our place.

Jesus alone paid all our debt,
and it's our assignment
to love and protect;
our sisters, our brothers,
that some would condemn,
never letting up about their sin.

We ought to strive to spare them,
from the enemy's voice, vented by men,
Crying;
"Crucify, Crucify, Crucify Them!"

Our Heavenly Hope
****

Unlike man, God's mercy endures forever.

Ephesians 2:4-6
"But God is so rich in mercy,
and he loved us so very much,
that even while we were dead
because of our sins,
he gave us life
when he raised Christ from the dead.
(It is only by God's special favor
that you have been saved!)
For he raised us from the dead along with Christ,
and we are seated with him
in the heavenly realms—
all because
we are one with Christ Jesus." 1

I KNOW YOU BETTER THAN YOU THINK
(Battling an accuser)

God's elect, His special ones
will be opposed and critically shunned.
Eliab, David's oldest brother said;
"I heard you speaking with the men."
In anger, he asked David; "Why have you come?"
"And what about your sheep,
who's caring for them?"

"Oh, I know how conceited you are,
and how wicked is your heart."

I KNOW YOU BETTER THAN YOU THINK!

But, did Eliab ever stop to think
he's jealous, conceited, angry, unkind—
to God's chosen vessel, in God's chosen time?

Did Eliab ever really stop to think,
He touched one of God's priceless sheep.
One destined to smash all of those,
who come against the people God chose.

That's what a self-exalting spirit will do,
condemn the sheep
that challenge them to—
stand up and fight a giant or two.

Maybe the real giant David fought that day
was his accusing brethren and what they had to say!

David didn't seek to be in the lime light,
He knew it was God's will,
and he knew it was God's fight.

Our Heavenly Hope
****

God is on our side.

Psalm 118:5-6
"I called upon the Lord in distress:
the Lord answered me,
and set me in a large place.
<u>*The Lord is on my side;*</u>
I will not fear:
what can man do unto me?"

When others point, accuse, condemn,
God will lift us UP again!

Psalm 71:20
"You have allowed me to suffer much hardship,
but you will restore me to life again
and lift me up
from the depths of the earth." [1]

INVISIBLE NAILS
(Battling sin)

Nails in thee, nails in thee—
so invisible, these nails in thee.

Blow by blow, they're driven in,
wounds so deep, these nails within.

Those You love, who break Your heart,
as they turn from God and His Word depart.

We put nails in thee, nails in thee—
so invisible, these nails in thee.

All the times I've let you down,
failed to trust, and messed around.

Words spoken, not in love,
aimed to hurt and trying to be tough.

I put nails in thee, nails in thee,
so invisible,
these nails in thee.

Our Heavenly Hope
****
He is faithful to forgive.

1 John 1:9
"If we confess our sins, he is faithful and just
to forgive us our sins, and to cleanse us
from all unrighteousness."

ENCOMPASSED BY NIGHT
(Battling the darkness within)

Behind an enormous door there lies,
blackness so dark I'm paralyzed.
Why am I encompassed by night?
And what has happened to my light?

Feeling perplexed and so alone,
I wonder how could one ever atone,
for their awful blackened state?
How, God, will I ever escape?

Why would God open my eyes to see,
a darkness so gross,
that it overwhelms me?
I learn of His Grace as I come to my end,
No longer by self,
I am depending on Him.

As He reveals things to me in the dark,
rays of pure HOPE
pierce through my heart.
He's teaching that He alone
creates the light and the dark,
He redeems, He restores, and
He never departs.

I'm learning to wait and to trust Him more.
As I stand and knock; Soon,
He'll open the door.
And when I finally step into His light,
I'll be His ray, to those—Encompassed By Night!

****

Micah 7:7-9
"As for me, I look to the Lord for his help.
I wait confidently for God to save me, and my God
will certainly hear me.
Do not gloat over me, my enemies!
For though I fall, I will rise again.
Though I sit in darkness,
the Lord himself will be my light.
I will be patient as the Lord punishes me,
for I have sinned against him.
But after that, he will take up my case
and punish my enemies
for all the evil they have done to me.
The Lord will bring me out of my darkness
into the light,
and I will see his righteousness." [1]

Even as Christians we sin against the Lord.
The difference is that after our correction
or season of judgment is passed,
He brings us through the dark times and into the light.
He uses those dark times in our souls passage
to get us to focus on His Righteousness
and not our own.
Unlike man, His judgments are for us
(they benefit us),
his corrections are always
for our good.

****

His Character! His Righteousness!
He is faithful, forgiving,
and He delighteth in mercy!

Micah 7:18-19
"Who is a God like unto thee,
that pardoneth iniquity,
and passeth by the transgression
of the remnant of his heritage?
he retaineth not his anger forever,
because he delighteth in mercy.
He will turn again,
he will have compassion upon us;
he will subdue our iniquities;
and thou wilt cast all their sins
into the depths of the sea."

WE HAVE PEACE WITH GOD
(Battling unforgiveness)

What do you think robs our peace within?
Maybe it's those that have been forgiven
and forget where they've been.
He came not to judge or condemn,
and as you forgive, so shall you be forgiven.
God alone can help us see
the Word of God, THE PLAN,
is to forgive, and to grant reconciliation.

If you allow Him to deal with all who offend
He won't need to point and say;
"Sorry, you may not enter in, for you too are unforgiven."

Don't just say it with your lips
out of duty or pious pretentiousness.
God sees into the heart of man
and only God The Almighty can, by His grace
make anyone of us to stand!

Our Heavenly Hope
****
We have peace with God.

Romans 5:1-2
"Therefore being justified by faith,
we have peace with God
through our Lord Jesus Christ:
By whom also we have access by faith
into this GRACE wherein we stand,
and rejoice in hope of the glory of God."

USURPEE
(Battling popular opinion)

There's a cost should you choose to be,
known as a Usurpee.
A sheep that speaks against the wrong,
who dares to challenge an unholy throng—
of those who hate, condemn, despise,
the imperfect people for whom Christ died.
There's a cost should you choose to be
known as a Usurpee.
To confront loveless, immature men,
Declaring that Jesus came,
not to oppress, judge or frame,
imperfect people—
WE'RE ALL THE SAME!
We all need forgiveness, and restoration.
My sheep know my voice, they know how I care—
they won't be destroyed, by wolves unaware.
It's the Love of God that they listen to,
not a verbal stoning or a manipulative few.
The Lord will deliver them
from the venomous words of mean, angry men.
Then God grants his power to be
a bold sheep that speaks, a Usurpee.

Our Heavenly Hope
****

The sons of God (matured Christians) are not led by
popular opinion—they are led by The Spirit of God!

Acts 5:29
***"Then Peter and the other apostles answered and
said, We ought to obey God rather than men."***

NOTHING
(Battling discouragement)

Nothings going to stop me from going after You.
No matter what men say, Lord, no matter what they do.

My mind is not focused on the opinions of men,
for I'm an overcomer and I'm rising up again.

By compassion I'll be driven; Your love Lord, to impart
for I have been given a broken, contrite heart.

I'll go all the way, Lord; no matter what the cost,
no matter if I fail God, no matter if I'm lost.

I know that You are there, Lord; and always will be,
so absolutely NOTHING, Lord, is going to stop me!

Our Heavenly Hope
****
God always finishes what He starts.

Psalm 138:8
"The Lord will perfect that which concerneth me..."

Hebrews 12:2
*"Looking unto Jesus, the author
and finisher of our faith;..."*

Nothing's over till He says it's over—

John 19:30
"...It is finished:..."

PASTOR PLEASE DON'T!
(Battle for complete restoration)

Pastor,
Please don't take it off,
I don't want to see,
to see, the real ugly me.

Pastor,
Please don't reveal that
hidden defect,
how could it serve, to do that?

Pastor,
Please don't open up that can of worms,
it makes us wiggle, it makes us squirm.

Pastor,
Please don't remove that robe of sin,
nakedness is just not in.

Pastor,
Please don't go there,
people just might start to stare.

Pastor,
Please don't point out,
that I'm not trusting God
if I'm just befriending doubt.

Pastor,
Please don't stay too long,
you might just uncover
all that's wrong.

Our Heavenly Hope
****

God may use a man to expose our sin but,
He does not stop there—
God cleanses and covers, redeems and restores.

Let us pray
that we too can go beyond
merely
pointing and accusing,
and that we can also learn to
wash our brothers and sisters dirty feet
in gentleness and fear,
aware that it might be us one day
at the end of a pointed finger or remark.

Galatians 6:1-2
"Brethren, if a man be overtaken in a fault,
<u>*ye which are spiritual,*</u>
restore
such an one in the spirit of meekness;
considering thyself,
lest thou also be tempted.
Bear ye one another's burdens,
and so fulfill
the law of Christ."

God's love brings attention to what's wrong
but His motive is to completely heal
and cover us from the effects of sin and shame.
Because if we can not get past the sin, we merely stir up
strife rather than lovingly restore someone.
Proverbs 10:12
"Hatred stirreth up strifes:
but love covereth all sins."

MIRROR, MIRROR
(Battling pride)

"<u>Mirror, mirror on the wall,
who's the most spiritual
of us all</u>?"

Is it the one who advises the most?
Or the one in the lime light
that everyone toasts?

Is it the mother with perfect kids
all serving the Lord;
What is written,
What saith the Lord?

Is it the one who admits
the most serious faults,
or the sleaziest sins?
Or the one who embraces
all of them?
Aren't they so special,
so tolerant?
Or maybe luke-warm
or indifferent.

Mirror, mirror on the wall;
come on, I'm ready,
tell me all!

Is it the one
with a heart like His?
And who's job is it
to judge this?

Is it the one who keeps the leaders appraised;
"There's sin in the camp,
Surprise! Surprise!"

Mirror, mirror on the wall,
who is the most spiritual of us all?
That can't be true,
You say,
"NONE AT ALL!"

"What?"
"We are all equal in His eyes?"
"What?"
"There's not one special one;
I'm horrified!"

I thought I might have something special,
something new.
I thought you might say,
"Yes, It could be you!"

"Mirror, mirror on the wall—
Who asked you,
after all!"

Our Heavenly Hope
****
Jesus saves all sinners, even the proud.

1 Timothy 1:15
"This is a faithful saying,
and worthy of all acceptation,
that Christ Jesus came into the world
to save sinners; of whom
I am chief."

A STATUE IN THE MIDST
(Battling for freedom)

From one ungodly attack to another,
no real help from a sis or a brother.
Trying to escape the hurt and the pain,
trying to protect myself and maintain—
my life and my security, as well as my obscurity.

It's odd to be in your enemies midst,
learning to coexist as a separatist.
Knowing that they can't see the real you,
and that all they see is just a statue.
An image, you hope, they won't judge or demean—
a profile, you hope, is not too threatening.

It's not my idea or desire to create,
a stone, a heart that none can penetrate.
Nevertheless, here I stand, in an antisocial wonderland,
with all my hidden hopes and dreams,
with all my secret fears and silent screams.
My soul stands alone as it coexists
as a statue in the midst.

A spark of hope ignites my soul
as I pray, O God, I know You know!
You can make the changes in me,
You alone can set me free—
with one stroke of Your creativity—
I'll be the Master's Statue
of Liberty!

And as men gaze at this statue in their midst—
they may read a prayer like this:

Free me from the desire to sin
Free me from complacent men
Free me from the fears within
Free me from disillusionment
Free me from placing trust in men
Free me from pious pretentions
Free me from wanting to please
Free me from expecting ease
Free me from figuring it all out
Free me from vain spiritual bouts
Free me from all my self contempt
Free me from all I've ever dreamt
Free me from an ungrateful heart
Free me from my undone part
Free me from all of my unrest
Free me from all unfaithfulness
Free me from all that I don't see
Free me that I might serve only thee

And as men read this prayer
my prayer shall be—The Lord will bless them
with His artistry
and turn each one into His statues—
Statues of Liberty!

Our Heavenly Hope
****
John 8:36
"If the Son therefore shall make you free,
ye shall be free indeed."

MY FAITHFUL FRIEND
(Battling loneliness)

While in the fire of testing, Jesus visited me.
By natural eyes, the only thing that I could see
was total darkness encircling me.

I said; "I have no hope!" I was looking for a rope.
Won't someone see the pain in me?
Won't someone hug me please?
I was left to my own demise,
as unrelentlessly they criticized.
But, deep down in my heart,
a ray of hope would not depart.
I still had one faithful friend,
I knew on Him I could depend.

As I sat accused, condemned,
wondering how, wondering when,
The Lord will show to all of them,
His desire for mercy and restoration.

As dark and black as words could ever be
were their unkind words to me;
"We can't place a guard in the front
to keep you out.
But, if you care for people like you say,
you won't come back here,
you'll go away!"
But, Jesus had a plan,
He took me by the hand,
He walked me through the furnace,
And then He delivered me from all the venom
of mean, self-righteous men.

Our Heavenly Hope
****

So much greater is He that is in me,
so much greater is His righteousness,
So much greater is
My Faithful Friend,
in Him my hope shall rest!

Psalms 31:24
"Be of good courage, and he shall
strengthen your heart,
all ye that hope in the Lord."

A special scripture to pray for the comfort of others—

2 Thessalonians 2:16-17
"May our Lord Jesus Christ and God our Father,
who loved us
and in his special favor gave us
<u>everlasting comfort and good hope,</u>
comfort your hearts and give you strength
in every good thing you do and say." [1]

No matter how hopeless one may feel, the Word of God
declares that His comfort and His good hope
are everlasting.

It is when we believe the Word of God above and beyond
our personal feelings or thoughts
that we can truly be comforted in any situation.

I JUST WANT TO LOVE YOU THAT WAY
(Battle song)

I want to love You that way;
to fall at Your feet, to humbly display,
tears of thanksgiving for a new start,
with kisses proclaiming—
"You're The King of my heart!"

I want to love You that way;
to spend myself to bring relief,
to my Master's mighty feet.
Anointing the One I adore
with a broken heart, wanting nothing more—
than to love You my Lord.

I want to love You that way;
in sweet submission, as yielded clay,
only depending on what You have to say—
I just want to love You, O Lord, to love You that way.

Our Heavenly Hope
****
The Lord satisfies my deepest desire—to be close to Him.

Psalms 145:16-20
*"Thou openest thine hand, and satisfieth the desire of
every living thing. The Lord is righteous in all his
ways, and holy in all his works. The Lord is nigh unto
all them that call upon him, to all that call upon him
in truth. He will fulfil the desire of them that fear
him: he also will hear their cry, and will save them.
The Lord preserveth all them that love him: but all
the wicked will he destroy."*

A DIFFERENCE
(Battling an emotional stoning)

Wounded, wearied and worn,
emotionally bloodied and spiritually scorned—
I asked my Father who knows the good and the bad;
"Have I made a difference in your life, Dad?"

Deep inside I longed to know,
has my life mattered to even one soul?
I knew that I could truly depend
on Dad to be honest and open.
He didn't answer right there or right then,
he called me later to respond, saying quite encouragingly;
"Honey, you've made a difference,
you've made a difference to me!"

An encouraging wind blew over my heart,
knowing that I played a special part.
If I made a difference, a difference to him,
then I could make a difference to someone again.
Thank-you, Dad, for helping me see,
I count, I'm special, life is not vanity.

Our Heavenly Hope
****
The Lord binds up many wounds by sending us
verbally "Good Samaritans."

Psalms 147:2-3
"The Lord doth build up Jerusalem:
he gathereth together the outcasts of Israel.
He healeth the broken in heart,
and bindeth up their wounds."

WHAT WOULD MAMA SAY?
(Battling depression)

Up in glory with The Lord, what would Mama say now?
Would it be an encouraging word?
I believe it would be, somehow.
Maybe she would say; Listen closely, Laura Kay,
God only wants what's best for you!
Trust Him, He'll make things right for you.
Don't ever give up. That's exactly what old
Slew-Foot would want you to do. Remember the song;
I Believe—Believe—For every tear that flows,
A BLESSING GROWS!
Believe—For every storm that wails,
THE LORD PREVAILS!
Believe—For every depressing hour,
THERE IS A HIGHER POWER!
Believe—For every door slammed shut,
God is preparing to put you, child,
WHERE YOU NEED TO BE AT!
Believe—For every need or every plead,
HE IS ALL YOU'LL EVER NEED!
Believe— For every misplaced step
HE WILL GUIDE AND REDIRECT!
And **Believe**— My precious daughter,
YOUR IN THE HANDS OF AN ALMIGHTY POTTER!

Our Heavenly Hope
****
Depression often lifts by believing what God says.

Mark 9:23
*"Jesus said unto him, If thou canst believe,
all things are possible to him that believeth."*

42

APPLY THE EYESALVE PLEASE
(Battling confusion with prayer)

The Possible Prayer of Mary for John
O Lord, give John a vision so he can see,
apply the eyesalve of revelation knowledge please.
To those loyal loving eyes, who saw You brutally crucified.
And when he knows Your holy plan
touch him Jesus with Your right hand.
Still the doubts, the fears that rage,
cause him to write the final page.
Let him, Jesus, say it well—
Your awesome visions to unveil.
Proclaiming to all quite powerfully,
the final word, the victory.
In Jesus name I bow my knee, for the beloved
You've entrusted to me.

Our Heavenly Hope
****
John 14:14
"If ye shall ask anything in my name, I will do it."

The Apostle John (Mary's beloved) writes:
Revelation 1:17-19
"And when I saw him, I fell at his feet as dead.
And he laid his right hand upon me,
saying unto me, Fear not; I am the first and the last:
I am he that liveth, and was dead;
and behold, I am alive for evermore, Amen;
and have the keys of hell and of death.
Write the things which thou hast seen,
and the things which are,
and the things which shall be hereafter;"

THE ABC'S OF Y2K
(Battle plan)

A is for asking!
Ask and it will be given unto you.
Ask for divine wisdom
Ask for your daily bread
Ask for what you have need of
Ask for faith not to fail
Ask and it will be given unto you.

B is for being!
Be content with what you have
Be joyful in hope
Be patient in affliction
Be faithful in prayer
Be alert and watchful
Be expectant of God's providential care.

C is for coming!
Come and consider the lilies
Come and commit your plans unto the Lord
Come and I will give you rest
Come and bow down in worship
Come, let us adore Him.
Come, Lord Jesus, Come!

Our Heavenly Hope
****

When we believe that the Lord has a good plan
then our heavenly hope
cannot be shaken.

Psalm 33:11
"But the Lord's plans stand firm forever;
his intentions can never be shaken." 1

Proverbs 16:3
"Commit your work to the Lord, and then
your plans will succeed." 1

Proverbs 19:21
"You can make many plans,
but the Lord's purpose will prevail." 1

Hebrews 13:5,6
"Stay away from the love of money;
be satisfied with what you have.
For God has said,
I will never fail you. I will never forsake you.
That is why we can say with confidence,
The Lord is my helper, so I will not be afraid.
What can mere mortals do to me?" 1

Romans 12:12
"Be glad for all God is planning for you.
Be patient in trouble,
and always be prayerful." 1

Psalms 95:6,7
"Come, let us worship and bow down.
Let us kneel before the Lord our maker,
for he is our God.
We are the people he watches over,
the sheep under his care." 1

COURAGE TO SEE
(Battling insecurities)

Give me courage, Lord, so I can see;
empower me, Father, eternally,
to embrace Your word, Your plan,
to enable me to take a stand.

Give me courage, Lord, so I can see;
it's not my strength or understanding,
but it's faith and grace maturing me,
beyond confusions, doubts and insecurities.

Give me courage, Lord, so I can see;
You only want what's best for me.
You always teach, to lose is to gain,
Some losses, Lord, cause so much pain.

Give me courage, Lord, so I can see;
others can make it without me.
I'm not a Savior, I'm only a man,
trusting with my whole heart in Your plan.

Our Heavenly Hope
****

God's throne is called THE THRONE OF GRACE,
not the throne of law or legalism.

Hebrews 4:16
"Let us therefore come boldly unto
THE THRONE OF GRACE,
that we may obtain mercy,
and find grace to help in time of need."

46

I WILL NOT BE AFRAID
(Battling fear)

I will not be afraid of tomorrow
with it's hideous shame and sorrow.
Because tomorrow the sorrow will be
but a tool used to forge within me,
traits, character, and qualities;
Just like the one who's agony,
elevated Him to honor and victory!

I will not be afraid of the present
with it's in your face torrents.
Because present torrents that rage;
all preplanned and prearranged,
are like the One's who's torrents staged,
the noblest triumph ever made!

I will not be afraid of my past
with it's claws of failure that thrash.
Because past regrets, wounds and woes
are only tools of the One who knows;
that they will one day be truly known,
as precious, victorious, stepping stones.
From garbage to grace to glory—"I'm Home!"

Our Heavenly Hope
****
God uses the good, the bad, the garbage, and even the sad!
Romans 8:28
***"And we know that all things work together for good
to them that love God, to them who are the called
according to his purpose."***

TAKE IT OUT OF ME, LORD
(Battling bitterness)

Take it out, the fangs that pierce my heart
and vehemently tear me apart,
reminding me of all the hate.
Then help me, God to penetrate
into caverns where men art—
hiding all their bloodied hearts.

Heal, O God, the festering place,
so deep, so dark, so full of disgrace.
It hurts, take it out—just like in my dream
where you ripped out this snake, this ungodly thing.

I cry out like a child to You, Crying;
"Take it out, take it out, whatever You do.
And replace it, yes replace it,
replace it with You!"

Our Heavenly Hope
****
CHRIST is IN us!
He replaces our bitter thoughts with better ones.

Colossians 1:27
"For it has pleased God to tell His people
that the riches and glory of Christ
are for you Gentiles, too.
For this is the secret: Christ lives in you,
and this is your assurance
that you will share in his glory!" [1]

GRACE TO HOLD YOU
(Battling weaknesses)

As I seek direction I often find,
my biggest battle is here in my mind.
The more I try to see things clear,
the more my heart wrestles with fear.

My child;
Surrender to faith and let my grace hold you,
I'll shape and mend, love and mold you.

My grace gives you strength to step out in faith,
and my love always covers disgrace.
Proving mercy and grace are always greater
than all the laws and traditions created.

My child;
Surrender to faith and let my grace hold you,
I'll teach and bless, use and console you.

I want to show you it's me and not you,
that crowns with success and victory too.
So I placed a word inside of thee,

Saying;
"My grace is sufficient for thee!"

Our Heavenly Hope

****

When we are weak—He is strong!

2 Corinthians 12:9-10
"And he said unto me,
My grace is sufficient for thee:
for my strength
is made perfect in weakness.
Most gladly therefore will I rather glory
in my infirmities,
that the power of Christ
may rest upon me.
Therefore I take pleasure in infirmities,
in reproaches, in necessities, in persecutions,
in distresses for Christ's sake:
for when I am weak, then am I strong."

THE DOOR
(Battling blindness)

O, Lord, I desire the gift of a revelator.
Jesus, please open my mind, please open THE DOOR!
You can grant me eyes to see
and holy eyesalve to enable me
to enter in—to great riches in Him.
O Lord, I ask for the gift of
spiritual revelation.

I know You're the way, the truth and the life,
and only You open
THE DOOR of insights.
Allow me, O Lord, to give liberally,
all You've given unto me.
Open the door that no one can shut,
that I may guide all that You put,
in my path as I journey in The Spirit.
Amen

Our Heavenly Hope
****
We have available to us holy eyesalve—The Word of God!
The more we apply this salve, the more
we see in The Spirit.
We see that Jesus is not only our Great Physician—
He is our Great Ophthalmologist!

Revelations 3:18
"I counsel thee to... anoint thine eyes
with eyesalve that thou mayest see."

THE NAME OF THE GAIN
(Battling materialism)

Excited, envious, enamored, enthralled,
asking, aching, amazed, and appalled.
People lusting, laboring in pain,
every day a new struggle in vain.

Striving, slaving, scheming, screaming,
yesing and yearning, a yelp and a yawn.
For what? Why? What's going on?
Hang-ups, hassles, hiccups, HELLO?
Anyone out there? Anyone know?

We're wishing, wanting, willing, and wandering,
then flippant, flat, flustered, and floundering.
We're goofing and guessing; we gossip and grump,
we're deceiving, deluding, we doubt and we dump—
our complaints, contentions, corny clichés,
our blurred boastings and our belly-aches.

People scurrying, laboring for gain;
grant us Your wisdom to see once again.
It's all to bring man down on his knees.
To fear forever, The Father who sees,
our blind, empty struggle and strain—
now, here's
"The Name of The Gain,"
to replace it all with God's gracious gifts;
OF
GODLINESS AND CONTENTMENT!

Our Heavenly Hope

****

God's secret to great success is
godliness with contentment.

1 Timothy 6:5-6
"Perverse disputings
of men of corrupt minds, and destitute of the truth,
supposing that gain is godliness:
from such withdraw thyself.
But godliness with contentment is great gain."

THE MESS
(Battling oppression)

Oppressed, stressed, vexed and perplexed,
fear and grief, grip and test,
confusion and chaos—what a mess!

My mind and reason, who will redeem?
An awful season and an awful scene.
I try again and again,
only to discover that I'm lost within.

Is it a curse related to sin?
Or a special judgement for failing,
His voice within?

Our Heavenly Hope
****

Unlike all the other religions of the world—
We Know Our Redeemer Lives!
And because He lives we can face any oppression with
confidence! Job was the most oppressed man in the bible
but he found hope and comfort in the knowledge
that his Redeemer lives;

Job 19:25-26
*"For I know that my redeemer liveth,
and that he shall stand at the later day
upon the earth: And though after my skin
worms destroy this body,
yet in my flesh shall I see God:"*

His hope was stronger than his hurt!

54

THE SOLUTION
(Battling the mess)

Trust and wait on Him
for your answers or interpretations.
Allow His words inside your heart
to speak—to the waves impart,
words that honor His holy name,
then you shall see an awesome change.

Say no to sneaky, creepy ideas that invade.
Say yes to solutions that never fade.
No matter the mess, the grief or the test,
In His words—there is a rest.

Don't put your trust in men or flesh,
give it to God and you'll be blessed.
Don't try to figure what, why, or when.
Trust and wait upon Him,
for Him to bring
your solution.

Our Heavenly Hope
****
Good/godly things come to those who wait!

Psalms 33:20-21
"Our soul waiteth for the Lord:
he is our help and our shield.
For our heart shall rejoice in him,
because we have trusted
in his holy name."

When the enemy attacks our hope
with creepy ideas,
like; "There is no hope."
Our greatest defense is what we believe.
Do we really believe that
God will deliver us from all afflictions?

Psalms 34:19
"Many are the afflictions of the righteous:
But the Lord delivereth him
out of them all."

DREAMING AGAIN
(Battling the skeptics)

I dare to believe in every dream
knowing that God creates everything.
No devil ever made or revealed
the secrets that the Lord conceals.

For those who place their trust in Him
won't be deceived or deluded.
It's when we put our trust in men
that we are deceived and deluded.

Those who are jealous,
who hate and condemn
special ones inspired by Him;
should know that God's Word
clearly points out
that only God has the spiritual clout,
to judge the dreams faithfully told,
to assess the motives of those so bold,
to declare an unbelievable dream,
to those who criticize everything.

I've heard it said dreamers are egotists,
mentally ill and probably obsessed.
Well, I dare to believe God's Holy Word,
and I choose to follow my Shepherd,
He told me and He told you;
"My sheep hear my voice."
And that's the truth!

Our Heavenly Hope
****

God still speaks to His sheep.

Job 33:14-16
"For God speaketh once, yea twice,
yet man perceiveth it not.
In a dream, in a vision of the night,
when deep sleep falleth upon men,
in slumberings upon the bed;
then
He openeth the ears of men,
and sealeth their instruction,"

YAWNING THE BLUES
(Battling spiritual neglect)

As I sat in the pew listening to you
I felt the sting of a whip
words that abuse.
Words that accuse are words that lose
respectful attention
and I began yawning the blues.

Curled up on my bed tears flow
from a heart that's sad.
Where is the love, and where does one go,
to be relieved from belittling pros?

Yes, some know how to define
the Greek and Hebrew—
but really they don't always know
or care about you.

You make mistakes
so off—you go to confess
hoping for shepherdly guidance.
Behind your back they spread the news—
those pros who despise the likes of you.
So here I go yawning the blues.

Our Heavenly Hope
****
Time heals some things, but God's love heals everything.

Romans 13:10
"Love does no harm to it's neighbor..." 2

Our Heavenly Hope

****

When those in leadership neglect our spiritual
development or worse,
when their indifference causes us to go backwards—
God steps in and provides the right amount
of discipline and love.

Ezekiel 34:15-16
*"I myself will tend my sheep and cause them to lie
down in peace, says the Sovereign Lord. I will search
for my lost ones who strayed away; and I will bring
them safely home again. I will bind up the injured
and strengthen the weak. But I will destroy the fat
and the powerful. I will feed them,
yes—feed them with justice!"* [1]

Some may feel that this poem is problematic in that it
might cause some to take license to quit going to church,
or to become critical of leadership, however there needs to
be balance. To say spiritual neglect is not an issue is a lie.
Leadership needs to take a look at how a sheep that has
been beat up feels so that leadership can
reach out to the spiritually neglected/abused ones.

And the sheep, myself included, must stay faithful to the
church and to their leadership as long as that church
and that leadership stay in submission to Christ.

I give special mention and honor to my current pastor,
Bob Miller of Faith Temple.
His ability to express truth and love has restored my faith
in quality leadership.
He is truly a pastor after God's own heart!

Our Heavenly Hope
****

There is no excuse for leaving the body of Christ.
Many leave the safety of Christian fellowship
because they feel so guilty about certain sins,
however, God gives a promise to restore you
and provide you with pastors after His own heart.
So don't let the enemy of your soul divide you from the
body, but, hang on to God's promises
of mercy and restoration.

Jeremiah 3:14-15
*"Turn, O backsliding children, saith the Lord; for I
am married unto you: and I will take you one of a
city, and two of a family, and I will bring you to Zion:
And I will give you pastors according to mine heart,
which shall feed you with knowledge and
understanding."*

Again, I say that when others desert or abandon us,
God is our help!

Jeremiah 17:17
"Lord, do not desert me now!
You alone are my hope in the day of disaster." 1

DEFENDING THE DEFENSIVE
(Battling defensiveness)

On Guard!
Take out your sword!
There will be a just reward.
To defend the defensive man, one must first understand,
he didn't get that way over night,
he was damaged, let down, affright.

What makes a mouth sarcastic, defensive, or unwhole?
What's lurking in such a soul?

We should look past our brethren's defensive mask
and see that maybe, within a defensive heart,
is a wounded warrior that's been picked apart.

Maybe if we would defend, protect, sustain
our brother's worth might be regained.
He wouldn't have to stand and say
It's untrue,
I'm not that way!

Our Heavenly Hope
****
The Lord is our defender.

Jeremiah 1:19
"And they shall fight against thee;
but they shall not prevail against thee;
for I am with thee, saith the Lord,
to deliver thee."

IN HIM
(Battle-front)

In Him we have an inheritance,
we are a divine display.
In Him we are creatively changed,
day after day after day.
He does not build a billion dollar estate in one night,
He clears the land, lays the foundation,
and places our walls upright.

He adds the windows, the doors,
He even paints walls and carpets floors.
He delights in setting in order
the house of His devout.
He loves to see His handiwork
and workmanship throughout.
Every piece of furniture has it's special place,
every picture and nick-knack,
all gifts of His grace.

As we dine in the kitchen we may hear Him
tapping on our hearts door
wanting to come in.
He loves to see how you'll react
or what you will say
about all the blessings
He gave as you obeyed.

You go to bed and find sweet rest unto your soul,
You realize a place in Him
we can all go.

As you sip from the cup of blessings
on your front porch swing,
reporters, friends, and family, all come
to ask you a few things.
They ask; "How did you inherit
this estate built by the Son?"
Then it dawns on you
as the light shines from within—
You begin to declare
what a gracious God will do,
for all repentant sinners, just like you.
Then you break out in a praise attack
and your guests just can't wait to come back.
They all want to see—what Jesus will do next in thee!

Our Heavenly Hope
****
God not only lives in us—
He builds us up into a holy temple.

Ephesians 2:19-22
"So now you Gentiles are no longer strangers and
foreigners. You are citizens along with all of God's
holy people. You are members of God's family.
We are His house,
built on the foundation
of the apostles and the prophets.
And the cornerstone is Christ Jesus himself.
We who believe are carefully joined together,
<u>becoming a holy temple for the Lord</u>.
Through him you Gentiles are also joined together
as part of this dwelling
where God lives by His Spirit!"

Ridden by Him
(Battling submission)

It was foretold, the king will come,
gently into the heart of Jerusalem.
On a wild, headstrong one,
ridden by Him, and Him alone.

So He comes to each man as Master,
grooming and training
for now and hereafter.
But it's the wild donkey inside of me
that He rides
till He reigns—most deliberately.

He makes us rejoice,
He makes us to see,
He's no longer riding
a willful donkey.

Soon The Faithful One who is True:
will be riding back on a brand new,
steed—a white horse of war,
with the armies of heaven,
as
The Final Victor.

He will ride victoriously in;
one last ride to destroy all sin.
Then it will be known by all men;
He changes His donkeys to proud prancin—
horses of war all
Ridden By Him!

Our Heavenly Hope
****

God is faithful and true
and He will return for me and for you.

Revelation 19:11-14
"And I saw heaven opened,
and behold, a white horse;
And He that sat upon him was called
Faithful and True,
And in righteousness he doth judge and make war.
His eyes were as a flame of fire,
and on his head were many crowns;
And He had a name written,
that no man knew, but He himself.
And He was clothed with a vesture dipped in blood:
And His name is called The Word of God!
And the armies which were in heaven followed Him
upon white horses,
clothed in fine linen, white and clean."

But when He returns He will not be
riding on or with untrained donkeys.

So DO I
(Battling repentance)

I had a terrible dream, my family all rebelled,
my heart completely bloodied, my spirit overwhelmed.
Curled in a ball, crying in the night,
asking God for mercy, begging for their plight.
I could hardly breathe, the agony of this sight,
no words could give me comfort—
repentance might.

I remember shaking as I revealed this agony of soul,
It was beyond my comprehension,
Why God would grieve me so?

So as I wrote the details
of this ungodly scene,
I began to understand a few things;
The anguish of The Master, for His family,
The heartbreak of seeing what lies ahead
for those when rebellion—they choose
and all the special blessings
that they alone will loose.

The horror of their dishonor,
their shame and their disgrace,
and the power of The Lord,
to put them in their place.

The scorn has crushed my heart and His
And I can guarantee you this;
I have never felt any pain like this.

The spirit within me so troubled, so grieved
as I realized God's broken heart
is unrelieved.

Then these words He gave to me:
**As your heart broke for your children,
so does mine!
As your spirit grieves over their sinful state,
their rebellion,
so does mine!
As you felt so hysterical about
the dishonor and the disrespect
you didn't deserve,
so do I!
As your child is pregnant with sin,
in such a sad expectant state,
a state that dishonors their family,
brought on with intimacy with the world,
so are mine!**

**As you tried everything in your power
to get them to listen to godly counsel,
so have I!**

**As you desired that they only love God and do good,
so do I!**

**As you struggled to lovingly endure,
so do I!**

**As your child comes into your house
and takes things without permission,
so do mine!**

**As you felt so alone in the battle at times,
so do I!**

**As you transferred blessings (in the dream)
to another more yielded vessel
with child-like faith,
so do I!**

Our Heavenly Hope
****

How awesome that God would share
a glimpse of His heart-ache.
Could it be that He looks for comforters too?
What would dry his tear streaked face?
No words could bring Him comfort—repentance might.

Psalm 69:20
"Reproach hath broken my heart;
and I am full of heaviness:
and I looked for some to take pity,
but there was none;
and for comforters, but I found none."

Whatever it takes to be a comfort
to my Holy Father,
that's what my prayer shall be.
I think a life of submission—
would bring my God relief.

BIBLICALLY OR POLITICALLY CORRECT
(Battling current correctness)

Biblically Correct	Politically Correct
●We agree with God's standards of correctness	●We agree with the current standards (and we're not to sure who devised them)
●We believe that every word of The Holy Bible is from God and it brings us truth	●We believe truth has many shades and perspectives. Truth for you may not be truth for me
●We exalt the principles and teachings of our Savior: Jesus Christ	●We exalt the principles and teachings of our Savior: Tolerance
●We expect to be changed by the power of God at work within us	●We expect to change ourselves and others by the power of human thought and wisdom
●We fear God and therefore seek to obey Him by becoming; *biblically correct*	●We fear rejection and the label of <u>intolerance</u> and therefore seek the world's acceptance by becoming; *politically correct*

Our Heavenly Hope
****

We have God's word to make us currently correct!

2 Timothy 3:16,17
"All scripture is given by inspiration of God,
and is profitable for doctrine, for reproof,
<u>*for correction,*</u>
for instruction in righteousness:
That the man of God may be perfect,
thoroughly furnished unto all good works."

We are warned in The Word that a day will come when
people will no longer listen to what is
biblically correct!

2 Timothy 4:3,4
"For a time is coming when people will no longer
listen to right teaching. They will follow their own
desires and will look for teachers who will tell them
whatever they want to hear. They will reject the truth
and follow strange myths." [1]

PLACES IN GOD
(Battle dress)

First there is the shower, the water is so fine;
It cleanses, it refreshes, and renews your mind.
He pours out His favor, He spares you so much;
here in the shower, restored by His touch.

Then God takes the towel of human suffering,
and as you step out of the shower
and you start to sweat,
He blots and dries, humbles and tests.
This is the place we all hate the most,
as He vexes and perplexes, where we can't even boast.

He takes away your dreams and then He gives you His,
He shatters foolish pride so that you will not miss—
His grace and His righteousness.

Next He prepares you to be redressed
in spectacular garments of His righteousness.
This third place in God is truly the best,
being clothed by God, having past the test.
Completely dried off and readied to go,
prepared by the hand of the only One who knows
the time to move you to the next phase,
where God can finally, finally be praised.
It's here that God is truly blessed,
as we exude His very best.

****

Ezekiel 16:8-11
"Now when I passed by thee, and looked upon thee,
behold, thy time was the time of love;
and I spread my skirt over thee,
and covered thy nakedness:
yea, I sware unto thee,
and entered into a covenant with thee,
Saith The Lord God,
AND THOU BECAMEST MINE.
Then I washed thee with water;
yea, I thoroughly washed away thy blood from thee,
and I anointed thee with oil.
I clothed thee also with broidered work,
and shod thee with badgers' skin,
and I girded thee about with fine linen,
and I covered thee with silk.
I decked thee also with ornaments,
and I put bracelets upon thy hands,
and a chain on thy neck."

Our nakedness is symbolic of the state that God finds us
in. Everything we have ever done is exposed and our only
hope for being able to stand unashamed before such an
awesome/holy God is that He dresses us in
His robes/clothes of righteousness!
Jesus Christ also advises us to purchase
from Him special garments;

Revelation 3:18
"I counsel thee to buy of me...,
and white raiment, that thou mayest be clothed,
and that the shame of thy nakedness
do not appear...;"

More Heavenly Hope

****

Our garments are purchased by the currency of faith,
a faith that is alive and obedient to God's will.

ENDURING
(Battling weariness)

I had a dream where fire came out,
the words I spoke without a doubt,
were not my own, they were the Lord's.
With holy passion out they poured,
Upon the ears of all to hear,
An emphatic word, so urgent yet clear—
over and over this word He gave;
***"Those who endure till the end,
shall be saved!"***

I was amazed as I awoke;
For I knew it was not merely I that spoke.
I had a sense of a special appointing,
when all will see
His awesome anointing.

Right now I must endure this place,
I feel hemmed in, I feel displaced.
O, God, I hope that day will still come,
in spite of all I have or have not done.
More than life itself I want to be a story,
of a worthless life;
who gave God the glory!

Our Heavenly Hope

****

The key to endurance is disentangling ourselves with the
affairs Christ never appointed to us.

2 Timothy 2:3-4
"Thou therefore endure hardness,
as a good soldier of Jesus Christ.
No man that warreth entangleth himself
with the affairs of this life;
that he may please Him
who hath chosen him to be a soldier."

To bring God glory, we need to be a story
of an untangled life, now that pleases Christ.

PREGNANT AND EXPECTING
(Battling spiritual abortion)

I'm pregnant and expecting all pain and agony,
personally to express;
God's Son eternally.

I'm pregnant and expecting a word birthed from above,
to grow in me and to become His twins
of Hope and Love.

Our Heavenly Hope
****
Have you ever been given a special promise or prophetic
word? That is similar to being pregnant with a hope.
As your hope grows, so does your expectancy
that God will keep His promise.

The enemy comes in to abort your hope;
abort your expectation,
and abort your faith
that God will perform His special promise to you.

Psalm 39:7
"And now, Lord, what wait I for?
My hope is in thee."
If we place our hope in God alone—
No one can abort it!

Avoid spiritual abortion clinics—
those skeptical, naysaying, faithless people & places.
Those that would suck the life out of you and
start looking for Hope in all the right places.

PUSH
(Battling low self-esteem)

I cried unto the Lord and asked Him;
Grant me a word, Lord, of encouragement.
Sleep took over my worn out being and in a dream
God spoke saying;
"PUSH"
In my heart I knew what He meant—
PUSH, bear down, be spent!
You're giving birth; words to be sent,
that give hope
and encouragement.

As I realized that God's about to birth
an incredible ministry
upon the earth—
designed to set many captives free;
prepared by
The Master of Ministry—
then my flesh reared up and said;
"But I'm afraid, I'm so afraid, I'm afraid to push,
to be used in the forefront;
I'm not worthy, I'll be attacked—
I'm the weakest one, just look at my past!"

Now I happen to know as a Mom, as a nurse,
that labor is not the place to be,
with all it's painful writhing
and all the agony;
I must obey without a fuss
and just do it, just
PUSH!

Our Heavenly Hope
****

God provides our inner strength.

Ephesians 3:16
"That he would grant you,
according to the riches of his glory,
<u>to be strengthened with might</u>
<u>by his Spirit in the inner man.</u>" [1]

More Heavenly Hope
****

God is able to do far more than we can imagine or ask.
One of my favorite promises is—

Ephesians 3:20-21
"Now unto him that is able
to do exceeding abundantly
above all that we ask or think,
according to the power that worketh in us,
Unto him be glory in the church
by Christ Jesus,
throughout all ages, world without end.
Amen."

He is able. Even to heal the poorest self-esteem
and replace it with the richest Christ-esteem.
When we know, really know, and really believe what God
says about his chosen ones then we are richer
than all the Lotto winners put together.

We can PUSH more effectively when we truly believe—
I am the righteousness of God in Christ Jesus.
That is Christ-esteem in a nutshell.

79

THE MOTHER OF LIFE
(Battling grief)

Put this firmly in your mind—
you will grieve for a time.
This godless world will have a blast,
yet their joy will not last.
The Spirit has given The Mother Of Life,
to His church, to His wife;
A precious seed—it's called His Word,
It's about to come forth, about to be birthed.

When the baby is born things will change;
this precious life will erase memories of pain.
Your ache, your agony, will not abide;
your every desire will be satisfied.

When I see you again you will know,
the answers to questions that once vexed your soul.
Joy will be like a river overflowing it's banks;
you'll be overwhelmed and so full of thanks.

For now, ask The Father in my name,
for all you need so your joy will remain.
According to His will, pray it may be done—
watch as He delivers, watch as He comes.

As the church is the woman—The Mother of Life,
soon she'll deliver, the timing is right.
For The Father will declare, He will respond—
Saying "Woman, Behold!
Behold Thy Son!"

Our Heavenly Hope

****

Our sorrow shall be turned into joy.

John 16:20
"Verily, verily, I say unto you,
That ye shall weep and lament,
but the world shall rejoice:
and ye shall be sorrowful,
<u>*but your sorrow shall be turned into joy.*</u>*"*

MORE ABUNDANT HONOR
(Battling with dishonor)

My daughter had a dream,
honor was the theme.
She and I sat in the bleachers
in a far back space
of an auditorium where a beauty pageant
was taking place.

We were watching the contestants parade
in front of an unseen judge,
they each displayed,
all their beauty; yet I was amazed—
As Jesus came he took my hand
and ushered me in front of them.

He made His selection;
a nobody, seated in the last section.

I was so overwhelmed to be first place
my daughter said;
"All you could do
is lead them all in praise
and acclamation of His Grace!"

Our Heavenly Hope

****

God bestows honor on the most dishonorable
members of His family.
Why?
Because to renovate something,
you have to give it what it needs,
not necessarily what it deserves.

1 Corinthians 12:23-24
"And those members of the body,
which we think to be less honorable,
upon these we bestow
MORE ABUNDANT HONOR;
and our uncomely parts have
MORE ABUNDANT COMELINESS
for our comely parts have no need:
But God hath tempered the body together,
having given
MORE ABUNDANT HONOR
to the part which lacked:"

SOLOMON SAW
(Battling lovelessness)

Solomon's desire was birthed from above
to gloriously surround and save His true love.

**He didn't see her sinful state,
He saw her with His eyes of grace.**

And as Solomon saw his one special bride,
the gaze of Christ on His beloved abides.
His love is
intense, romantic, unending,
He spends His time
chasing, courting, attending.
Christ will return, His bride to claim—
eternally satisfying
with a Love that remains.
And forever as Solomon saw
His one special bride
the eyes of our Beloved
will always abide.

Our Heavenly Hope
****

God sees us not as we are but as we shall be,
His True Love—His Bride!

Isaiah 62:5
*"For as a young man marrieth a virgin,
so shall thy sons marry thee;
And as the bridegroom rejoiceth over the bride,
so shall thy God rejoice over thee."*

84

OVERWHELMING EYES
(Battling the fear of rejection)

I am in love and so is He,
there's not enough time in all eternity;
to see His Holy Eyes of Grace, or to lovingly embrace,
The One who covers my disgrace,
and brings me to His Holy place.

I am in love and so is He,
with the eyes of The One who overwhelms me.

Our Heavenly Hope
****

His love is everything we long for,
it only takes one good look to know—He is The One!

Song of Solomon 6:5
"Turn away thine eyes from me,
for they have overcome me:..."

In a dream, the Lord Jesus enabled me by His grace,
to look into His eyes. I was afraid at first because I knew
that as soon as I made contact, I would know exactly
where I stood. The purest love in existence gazed into my
eyes and instantly His eyes overwhelmed me.
Tears gushed down my cheeks and I pleaded with The
Lord saying; "I know this is only a dream, but I don't want
to go back, let me stay here with You."
The Lord smiled and spoke softly to my heart;
"Soon you'll be with me forever."
Just one look and the search was over.
I had found everything I could ever desire in just one look.

BREATHLESS
(Battling emptiness)

My heart is ravished from above,
captivated by your awesome love.
Abandoned in your arms,
no longer restless,
embraced by The One
who leaves me
BREATHLESS!

I'm awed when our spirits entwine,
intoxicating my soul with thine.
There's no greater pleasure,
no finer wine,
than when You place
Your Spirit in mine!

Lord, move upon me in power today,
Arise and anoint Your beloved I pray.
Blessed now and forever by Your graciousness,
O God, You make me so
BREATHLESS!

Our Heavenly Hope
****

The Lord's Love is intoxicating.
And it is my hope
to be caught living under the influence!

Song of Solomon 1:2
"Let him kiss me with the kisses of his mouth:
for thy love is better than wine."

FOREVER I'LL LOVE YOU
(Battling with praise)

Father,
You're the strength of my life, Lord,
Your my Awesome Creator,
Architect of my soul—
O my God, Forever I will love You.

Jesus,
You're the Light of my life, Lord,
Your my Sun and my Moon, Lord,
You're the Beam in my eyes—
O my God, Forever, I will love You.

Spirit,
You're the Fire within me,
You're the Presence of God
that the world longs to see—
O my God,
Forever I will love You.
Forever I will love You.
Forever I will love You. O Lord.

Our Heavenly Hope
****

Praise is a mighty weapon
especially when we are at the end of our rope.
Praise brings God into the situation
and wherever He is—there is our heavenly hope!

Psalm 24:7-8
"Lift up your heads, O ye gates;
and be ye lift up, ye everlasting doors;
and The King of Glory
shall come in.
<u>Who is this King of Glory?</u>
The Lord strong and mighty,
The Lord mighty in battle."

TOGETHER FOR GOOD
(Battling with faith)

Thank-You, Lord, Almighty!
For opening eyes by Your words to see;
Your creative power
cleverly working together for good
in this final hour,
as You said it would.

Our Heavenly Hope
****
We need to place our hope in God's creative power.

Psalm 121:2
"My help cometh from the Lord,
which made heaven and earth."

If we put our hope in God's creative genius,
God's goodness and God's faithfulness
then we can rest assured
that our faith is pleasing to God.

If we really believe that **all** things are at work
in our lives for a **good** purpose
then we can **hope** in the fact that God
has **a good plan** for us.

Jeremiah 29:11
"For I know the plans I have for you," says the Lord.
"They are plans for good and not for disaster,
to give you a future and a hope." [1]

89

THE LOVE OF CHRIST
(Battling insecurity)

I have full confidence in God
that when one fails or falters
God never alters
in His unfailing love
as our faithful friend above.

Our Heavenly Hope
****
If we lose confidence we only need a fresh
revelation of God's faithfulness.

1 John 5:14
*"This is the confidence that we have in him,
that, if we ask anything according to His will,
He heareth us:"*

It's a sure testimony of God's goodness
that he only listens to what's according to His will,
because if we had everything we would ask for—
we would all be in trouble.

If we've lost confidence—we've lost faith.
If we've lost hope—we've lost faith.
If we've lost an ability to trust—we've lost faith.
If we've lost faith—we need grace;
for it is impossible to please God without faith.

Hebrews 11:1
"Now faith is being sure of what we hope for..." 2

THE HARD PART
(Battling the wait)

The hard part really is to wait
as God sovereignly orchestrates,
all the changes to take place,
in me so I can radiate,
as His Masterpiece of Grace.

Our Heavenly Hope
****

Just think! One day we shall all be gloriously
transformed—into His likeness!
David...

Psalm 17:15
"As for me, I will behold thy face in righteousness:
I shall be satisfied, when I awake,
with thy likeness."

Job...

Job 14:14
"If a man die, shall he live again?
all the days of my appointed time will I WAIT,
TILL MY CHANGE COME."

John...

1 John 3:2
"Beloved, now are we the sons of God,
and it doth not yet appear what we shall be:
but we know that, when he shall appear,
<u>*we shall be like him;*</u>
for we shall see him as he is."

I can hardly wait. To be all that I can be—
to be made like him.

91

WE GIVE YOU ALL OUR DREAMS
(Battling the unknown)
Song by Barry Eugene Black

Lord, we lift your name on high;
Dedicate our lives to You,
And we give You all our dreams,
There is nothing more to do.

How majestic is your name;
How eternal is your love,
And we give you all our praise,
Like the heavens up above.

And Lord we praise You, praise You,
Praise You with all of our hearts.
And Lord we praise You, praise You,
Praise You with all of our hearts.

Our Heavenly Hope
****

If we place our God given dreams
safely in God's hands
and not naively into man's hands,
we avoid a lot of jealousy and hatred
by those less inspired.

Genesis 37:5
"And Joseph dreamed a dream,
and he told it his brethren:
and they hated him yet the more."

SUDDEN ABRUPT ENDS
(Battling repentance)

I have visions at times I hardly comprehend,
planes crashing, trucks smashing,
all sudden abrupt ends.
Once I saw a fire flare up and flash in my face,
one time—a hall light exploding
all over the place.

Once my small car, parked all alone,
was totally smashed.
I've even seen my husband's head getting bashed.
My God's crashing, He's smashing,
He's a fire that's flashing.
And He's determined to consume all that's not lasting.

He makes the point all-right! We better listen and attend,
to the God in charge of all sudden abrupt ends.

Our Heavenly Hope
****
Sometimes we need to pray for people who do not fear God
to have enough sense to fear God.

Proverbs 19:20,21,23
"Hear counsel, and receive instruction,
that thou mayest be wise in thy later end.
There are many devices in a man's heart;
nevertheless the counsel of the Lord, that shall stand.
The fear of the Lord tendeth to life:
and he that hath it shall abide satisfied;
he shall not be visited with evil."

ZOO LIFE
(Battling with characters)

Don't you just love God's earthly zoo?
Tigers and bears and creatures like you.
What animal might God use to speak about you?

A snake in the grass, a hippo or two,
A sly ole fox or monkeys that muse?
A beaver, a bug, a bird or a bee?

How do you think God sees—
the behaviors that you demonstrate?
A gentile dog or an apostate?
A ravenous wolf that chews up the flock?
An eagle that soars or a chicken that squawks?

Have you ever wondered what cage you'd be in?
With the laughing hyenas or Porky's pig-pen?
Are you a lion, roaming God's range—
stalking, devouring or clawing the game?
Or are you as gentle as a dove,
or rough as a bull that's had quite enough!

Do you withdraw like a turtle into your shell,
Or wither and die like a salted snail!
Maybe you're a leopard—never changing your spots,
or an aardvark seeking ants in wooded lots.
Maybe a giraffe with such a high, stiff neck,
or a woodpecker pecking where he ought not to peck!

A singing white whale, so content, so strong—
or a mammoth manatee barely floating along?

Maybe you're a porcupine,
sticking and picking people apart—
or maybe a fluffy white sheepie, after God's own heart.

How do you think God sees you
as He looks out over His earthly zoo?
I dare you to ask Him to reveal that to you!

Our Heavenly Hope
****

Jesus tells us how
we are supposed to battle with characters.

Matthew 10:16
"Behold, I sent you forth as
sheep in the midst of wolves:
be ye therefore wise as serpents,
and harmless as doves."

God reveals things in parables, riddles,
metaphors, and analogies.
What kind of riddle or parable would He tell about us?

In Genesis, chapter 49, Jacob describes
many of his sons as animals:
Judah is called a young lion or a mighty ruler.
Issachar is called a strong ass or a beast of burden.
Dan is called a snake in the grass.
Naphtali is called a deer let loose.

The redeemed of the Lord are called
calves loosed from the stall.

Malachi 4:2
"But for you who fear my name,
the Sun of Righteousness will rise with healing
in His wings.
And you will go free,
leaping with joy like calves
let out to pasture." 1

As we grow in the Lord He keeps us in a stall,
but there comes a time when
He lets His calves loose.
I often pray;
Lord, quit stalling and let me loose!
However, only the Lord knows
the right time to let us out to pasture.
Or the right time to set us in Ministry.

TRAITORS IN DISGUISE
(Battling betrayal)

Traitors are not open, they are disguised—
Plotting and planning your life to overthrow,
as seeds of jealousy, lying, and hatred are sown.

A Judas will never confront you face to face,
It's behind the scenes that they spread your disgrace.
Their hatred is covered with their lying lips,
so full of themselves, and their own righteousness.

What you must do, do it quickly, Christ once said,
He knew Judas was already dead,
to all He had displayed, and soon in the garden,
He would be betrayed.

Judas made himself the judge, in Christ's final hours,
He thought himself wise, he abused his powers.
He would not humble himself and repent,
so God lifted the hedge and passed divine judgment.
He will repay those who touch His servants,
His anointed ones, and His prophets.
Thus saith The Lord, I've seen it all.
I will arise and my enemies will fall.

Our Heavenly Hope
****
When one is betrayed,
they are indeed most blessed—for they have been chosen
to share in the sufferings of Christ.

Matthew 20:18
"Behold, we go up to Jerusalem;
and the Son of Man shall be
betrayed unto the <u>chief priests</u> and unto the <u>scribes</u>,
and they shall condemn him to death."

Another biblical example of betrayal—

Psalms 55:12-14
"For it was not an enemy that reproached me; then I
could have borne it: neither was it he that hated me
that did magnify himself against me; then I would
have hid myself from him: But it was thou, a man
mine equal, <u>my guide</u>, and mine acquaintance. We
took sweet counsel together, and walked unto the
house of God in company."

There's a little traitor in all of us.
There's the friend we run to the religious leaders about,
the husband we talk evil about, the wife we are unfaithful
to, the parent we cut off, the child we bad-mouth,
the employer we resent, and every sister or brother in
Christ that we would rather talk about than to
labor for in intercession.

The best way I've found to deal with betrayal
is to do what Jesus did in the garden of agony—
Give it to God The Father and
go beyond it to a better place; into the garden of grace.

HELP ME TRUST IN YOU
(Battling doubt)

Whenever I'm displaced;
Needing Your strong embrace,
Seeking a hiding place,
Help me trust in You.
My Lord, My God; Help me trust in You.

Whenever I'm afraid,
Needing Your power, Your aide,
Seeking a hidden place,
Help me trust in You.
My Lord, My God; Help me trust in You.

Your Wings encircle me.
Your Arms deliver me.
Your Eyes empower me.
I will trust in You.
My Lord, My God; I will trust in You!

Our Heavenly Hope
****
We can safely place all of our hope, our trust
and our confidence in God's Word.

Psalm 119:114,116
"Thou art my hiding place and my shield:
I hope in thy word.
Uphold me according unto thy word,
that I may live:
and let me not be ashamed of my hope."

LET ME ALONE
(Battling the desire to die)

Job was declared the most righteous man alive
Yet we read how he really wanted to die.

"When I say, My bed shall comfort me,
my couch shall ease my complaint,
then thou scarest me with dreams,
and terrifiest me through visions:
so that my soul chooseth strangling,
and death rather than life.
I loathe it;
I would not live always:
<u>LET ME ALONE;</u>
for my days are vanity.
What is man, that thou shouldest magnify him?
And that thou shouldest set thine heart upon him?
And that thou shouldest visit him every morning,
and try him every moment?
How long wilt thou not depart from me, nor
<u>let me alone</u>
till I swallow down my spittle?"
(Job 7:13-19)

Job wanted to know why The Lord would not ease up.
He wanted God to let him die because he thought that he
had nothing to live for.
Job thought that his meaning for living was destroyed
and without meaning (a purpose) why continue?
He would soon discover that his reason to live was to
declare awesome truths to hurting, hopeless people of how
God **never leaves** nor forsakes His children!

100

Our Heavenly Hope

****

God may allow everything we think is valuable
to be destroyed, but if we hang on,
He teaches us what really makes living worthwhile.
God alone can bring purpose and satisfaction
to our otherwise worthless/empty lives.

Dear Lord,
Bless each of us with a new insight,
a new vision, a new perspective
of how valuable we can become
as we yield our lives
completely
to You.

VICTOR'S WREATH
(From battle to victory)

At the end of my journey awaits a crown;
It sparkles and glistens, it's brilliance astounds.
As I bow before His Majesty's throne;
joy fills my heart, yet, not mine alone.
All of creation in unified praise, singing, proclaiming;
all the triumphs He gave.
Through all the battles He has shown,
it's by His power and His grace alone!
What an awesome sight to see—
all these crowns before The King.
My mind is filled with glorious peace,
as I lay my crown down at His feet.
How awesome that He made it for me,
And How awesome is My Victor's Wreath.

Our Heavenly Hope
****

A crown of righteousness is laid up (in heavenly storage)
for all that love His appearing.

2 Timothy 4:7-8
*"I have fought a good fight, I have finished my course,
I have kept the faith:
Henceforth there is laid up for me
a crown of righteousness,
which the Lord, the righteous judge,
shall give me at that day: and not to me only,
but unto all them also that love his appearing."*

What's not to love about seeing Him in all His glory!

YESTERDAY, TODAY, AND FOREVER
(Battling my mind)

Yesterday, Today, and Forever,
places of joy, reflection, and ever—
frightening to those who do not quite grasp
an Almighty God whose confirming
His presence in future, present and past.

So many hearts overwhelmed by fear,
failing to sense just how near
You were, You are, You ever will be—
O Precious Lord,
increase our faith in thee.

How kind You are to open my mind's eye
in a dream showing how troubled am I.
Extinguishing all the hurts of the past,
showing to me that they won't last.

How loving You are
to speak through a dream **TODAY**—
verifying Your presence, and confirming Your stay.
Because You've taken residence within,
TODAY is just one more chance to dwell in Him.

FOREVER is the guy that gets me the most,
he's lurking, evasive, he's vague and verbose.
He whispers, I wonder, my mind taxes and toils—
enemy thoughts sneaking, seeking, striving to soil,
my mind with the doubt: that God will always be,
ever present, ever loving, and ever
ALL THAT I NEED!

Our Heavenly Hope

****

Hebrews 13:8
"Jesus Christ is the same
yesterday, today, and forever." [1]

Because Christ never changes I have hope.
Why?
Because I can count on him;
to stay merciful,
to stay forgiving,
to stay all powerful,
to stay all knowing,
to stay in prayer on my behalf,
to stay a creative genius,
and
to stay with me
forever!

ALL WE NEED
(The battle belongs to God)

He is the King, He is the Lord.
Nothing's impossible, Nothing's too hard.
He alone rules in righteousness;
His flocks to guide, His lambs to bless.
He changes their hearts, He gives them new clothes,
He fights all their battles,
He smashes their foes.
His Almighty eyes see quite differently,
as He looks out over eternity.
He sees the day when we will all be,
just like Him, all royalty.
An era not marked by time,
where cares and fears are left behind.
Where our deepest desire is satisfied—
TO BE IN HIS PRESENCE, TO REMAIN AT HIS SIDE!
Where our love for Him can finally be freed,
where THE ALL IN ALL is
ALL WE NEED!

Our Heavenly Hope
****
God supplies all we need through Christ.

Philippians 4:19
*"But my God shall supply all your need
according to His riches in glory
by Christ Jesus."* 1

The key here is—your need will be supplied—
not necessarily your wishes.

MY GOD! MY GOD! WHY ME? WHY ME?
(Battling for your sanity)

Have you ever cried out, while suffering—
My God! My God! Why me? Why me?

At the school of saintly socks,
the world calls
the school of hard knocks—
what lessons are remembered best?
Answered questions that once perplexed?
Or grievous losses, aimed to vex?
We want to know from the saints
of seminary row—
Where is God when grief rocks your soul?

Do you wonder what God is trying to point out,
as He relentlessly ignores you and you cry out.
Does He send abusive counselors to you,
in your darkest hours, to criticize too?

What was taught that really stuck?
Did it come out of a book?
Or was it scorn and shame
or integrity challenged and pride tamed?

Tell me graduates if you know—
what kind of God
would let you suffer so?
So much rejection and so much loss,
hurt, disappointment, even a cross?
What would Job or Jesus say if we cried;
"My God! My God! Why me? Why me?"

Would it be a holy plan
to change the hearts and minds of men?
Or would it all be to make you
and me more like Him?

Our Heavenly Hope
****
My Lord, My God, it is true—
when we stop asking why is when we start trusting you!

Psalm 71:5
"For thou art my hope, O Lord God:
thou art my trust from my youth."

No matter the suffering or the pain
we are all saved by faith
(by placing all our hopes)
in Him!

Romans 8:24
"For we are saved by hope:..."

TRUST WHEN YOU CAN'T CONTROL
(Battling for control)

O How it must grieve, His Holy Soul;
when we won't surrender and we long to control.
O Trust, when you can't control,
Trust in God when you can't control.
Don't ever, ever, ever let go
of trusting God when you can't control.

Events, outcomes, we cannot create,
but we don't want to listen and we don't want to wait.
O Trust, when you can't control,
Trust in God when you can't control.
Don't ever, ever, ever let go
of trusting God when you can't control.

The darkest pain I've ever known, is seeing how
I just let go of trusting God
when I was not in control.

Our Heavenly Hope
****

Our Hope is in knowing that God is in control—not man!
Mark 4:39-41
"And he arose, and rebuked the wind,
and said unto the sea, Peace, be still.
And the wind ceased, and there was a great calm.
And he said unto them, Why are ye so fearful?
how is it that ye have no faith?
And they feared exceedingly, and said one to another,
What manner of man is this,
that even the wind and the sea obey him?" [1]

LEAST OF THESE
(Marguerite's Battle for the little guy)

Mom's passion in her later years
were for those bound up by fears.
Her heart always seemed to see,
Jesus reaching for the least of these.

Jesus, faithful, loving and kind
took her spirit, soul, and mind.
He alone could free her soul, now her longing is to go—
to be in His presence, to see His face,
to bow before
His Amazing Grace!

This one thing I truly believe,
standing before Jesus she'll hear, she'll receive;

"What you have done unto the least of these
you have done it unto me!"

And in my spirit, she responds;
"Oh my children, please gather around,
I wish to share one final word,
Jesus wants me to tell you, He wants this heard;"
My heart's desire is to be here with Him,
If you love and obey Him, we'll be together again.
Don't forget the sick, the hungry, those dying in sin,
every prostitute, drug addict, all that's within
your path, your grasp, to reach them for Him.
For Jesus has told me quite tenderly;

"It will be through my children that others go free!"

Our Heavenly Hope
****

God is faithful to remember the good we do.

Matthew 25:40
"And the King shall answer and say unto them,
Verily I say unto you,
Inasmuch as ye have done it unto one of
the least of these
my brethren, ye have done it unto me."

XERXES
(Battling for position)

Xerxes was married to Vhasti,
a queen, gone quite nasty.
She would not submit,
obey or come,
she became quite an embarrassment.

But God, had a plan for Xerxes the King,
He created the dilemma,
He staged the scene.
He stirred up the elders to advise—
Xerxes to take a new wife.

Vhasti was replaced with God's choice,
He groomed Ester with beauty
and gave her a voice.
He presented Xerxes with Ester the Jew,
a different race, a different social milieu.

He was anointed to love her body, spirit, and soul,
God anointed her with favor and gave her a role—
to save many lives from mean violent schemes—
to ironically, eternally, change a few things.

Let us take heed to God's Holy Voice,
to use all we have,
to become God's choice.
To submit, to obey, and to become,
a vessel of honor and salvation!

****

Ester's greatest quality was not her beauty,
it was her courage, her fear of God,
and her intercessor's heart.
God still raises to positions of power—
genuine intercessors.

Ester 8:3-6
"Now once more Ester came before the king,
falling down at his feet
and begging him with tears
to stop Haman's evil plot against the Jews.
Again the king held out the gold scepter to Ester.
So she rose and stood before him and said,
If Your Majesty is pleased with me
and if he thinks it is right, send out a decree
reversing Haman's orders to destroy the Jews
throughout all the provinces of the king.
For how can I endure
to see my people and my family
slaughtered and destroyed?" 1

Ester did not focus on her position
or even her life,
she was only focused on doing
what was right.

WHO'S REALLY RUNNING THE SHOW?
(Battling for power)

When we are neglected, rejected,
and highly suspected,
When we are cut down, cut off, made a laughing stock,
When we are wounded and weary
becoming most leery,
When we falter and fail,
stumbling down the wrong trail

WHEN WE ARE RUNNING THE SHOW

God wants us to know;
that we grieve His holy soul
when we won't trust Him and vainly try
running the show.

Our Heavenly Hope
****
So often we think we are really trusting God
until He creates/allows a situation
beyond our control.
<u>Our hope rests in the fact that</u>
<u>God is really running the show.</u>

Psalms 103:19
"The Lord has established his throne in heaven,
and his kingdom rules over <u>all</u>." 2

I FEEL YOUR PRESENCE
(Battling dryness)

I feel your presence, I feel you here—
You have my heart, Lord, You have my ear.
I feel your presence and joy fills my soul,
a peaceful contentment, your chosen ones know.

I feel your presence—so holy and pure,
changing, conforming, us by your word.
I feel your presence, a holy desire,
to worship your highness, to be filled with your fire.

I feel your presence, each day within,
and there's no greater blessing,
no greater blessing, no greater blessing,
than being with Him!

Our Heavenly Hope
****
God's always changing things for the better.
He gives the weak strength, the troubled peace;
He turns mourning into dancing, grief into gladness and
depressing silence into heart-felt praise and worship.
Psalm 29:11
*"The Lord will give strength unto his people;
the Lord will bless his people with peace."*
Psalm 30:11-12
*"Thou hast turned for me my mourning into dancing:
thou hast put off my sackcloth, and girded me with
gladness; To the end that my glory may sing praise to
thee, and not be silent. O Lord my God,
I will give thanks unto thee for ever."*

QUENCH THIS
(Battling vexation of spirit)

It's true that a man's spirit may be vexed,
But nothing I know can ever
QUENCH THIS:

God's Pure Love

//
"Many waters cannot quench (God's) Love;
rivers cannot wash it away." 2
//
(Song of Solomon 8:7)

When emotional waters try to overflow me—
His love remains.
When hellish forces try to flush me out—
His love restrains.

Many waters cannot quench Him.
He cannot be stopped.
Neither can many rivers ever rinse Him off!

Yes, you can vex this spirit in me,
I can be dismissed.
But, no man can ever, ever, ever
QUENCH THIS:

His Eternal Loving Gift!

Our Heavenly Hope
****

<u>**Nothing**</u> shall ever separate us from the love of Christ!

Romans 8:33-39
"Who shall lay anything to the charge of God's elect?
It is God that justifieth. Who is he that condemneth?
It is Christ that died, yea rather, that is risen again,
who is even at the right hand of God,
who also maketh intercession for us.
Who shall separate us from the love of Christ?
shall tribulation, or distress, or persecution,
or famine, or nakedness, or peril, or sword?
...Nay,
in all these things we are more than conquerors
through him that loved us.
For I am persuaded, that neither death, nor life,
nor angels, nor principalities, nor powers,
nor things present, nor things to come,
Nor height, nor depth,
nor any other creature,
shall be able to separate us
from the love of God,
which is in Christ Jesus our Lord." [1]

HEAL THE LAND
(Battling for final restoration)

//
God wounds and God heals!
//
It is the Lord and not man,
who can compass
who can command—a suffering soul
in need of peace
who heals the humble, who brings relief.

God is at work in all our pain,
transforming us to be like Him.
To trust when we can't control,
leaving decisions to the One who knows,
what's best, what's wise, in these last days,
and when we meet Him,
we'll stand amazed.

That's why all creation groans,
it's an inner desire
To Go Home!

For it is JESUS
that will heal the land
in the Garden of Grace
where the Tree of Life stands.
By the leaves for all nations
we'll be whole once again.

Our Heavenly Hope
****

Jesus Christ is our Tree of Life.
And it is the leaves off His tree whereby all nations
will receive their final healing.

John 11:25-26
"Jesus said unto her,
I am the resurrection and the life:
he that believeth in me, though he were dead,
yet shall he live:
and whosoever liveth and believeth in me
shall never die."

Exodus 15:26
"For I, the Lord, am your healer."

Check this scripture out!
Revelation 22:1-2

MAHALO
(Battle Thanks)

I prayed one day not long ago;
teach me Lord to just let go
of my serious side
that I might know—all you've created,
a most spectacular show.
Mahalo!

I find when I focus on all the good
my heart enlarges
as Christ said it would.
I see the way God cares for me,
I'm warmed by the Sun, wooed by the breeze—
He slows me down, these moments to seize.
Mahalo!

Then, I learn to adore the seashells all so unique
dotting the seashore beneath my feet.
Oh, Abba Father, Ancient of Days,
You're altogether lovely, I stand amazed.
Mahalo!

Our Heavenly Hope
****

As fun as it is to spend a day at the beach,
collecting unique seashells—that cannot compare with
a day in His Presence
collecting the words or the wisdom of God that
He washes ashore unto my soul.
Mahalo!

2 Corinthians 2:14
**"But thanks be to God, who always leads us in
triumphal procession in Christ
and through us spreads everywhere the fragrance
of the knowledge of him."** 2

(Mahalo means thank-you in Hawaiian)

MY PRAYER ROSE TO YOU
(Battling total hopelessness)

///////////////////////////////////
There is HOPE
For the HOPELESS
///////////////////////////////////
If God can save a backslidden prophet
from the belly of a fish—
I know there's **nothing** too hopeless for God.

From inside the fish Jonah prayed to the Lord his God.
He said;

Jonah 2:1-9
"In my distress I called to the Lord,
and He answered me.
From the depths of the grave I called for help,
and You listened to my cry.
You hurled me into the deep,
into the very heart of the seas,
and the currents swirled about me;
all your waves and breakers swept over me. I said, I
have been banished from Your sight;
yet I will look again toward Your holy temple." 2

No matter how threatening
your present situation seems—there is HOPE!
"The engulfing waters threatened me,
the deep surrounded me;
seaweed was wrapped around my head."

The greater the sink—the greater the save!
"To the roots of the mountains I sank down;
the earth beneath barred me in forever.
But You brought my life up
from the pit, O Lord my God!"

Sometimes you have to lose life in order to find it.
"When my life was ebbing away
I remembered You, Lord, And
<u>*My prayer rose to You,*</u>
To Your holy temple."

He not only redeems and resurrects,
He also refocuses our priorities.
"Those that cling to worthless
idols (people, places, or things)
Forfeit the grace (favor) that could be theirs."

Having hope restored produces an attitude of gratitude.
"But, I with a song of thanksgiving,
will sacrifice to you."

True restoration produces faithfulness.
"What I have vowed I will make good."

And ultimately we learn that only God can save us.
"Salvation comes from The Lord!"

Maybe Jonah's song of thanks went like this—

Thank-You my God for delivering me
From worthless idols and coveting,
And all my rebellious backslidings.
Even though I sank so deep,
Your priceless grace restored me!
Men may never see,
How much attention that You took,
to get me to write this book.

A PERSONAL PORTRAIT OF HOPE
(Three great reasons to have hope)

The story of Jonah was my story.
I believed and confessed
that Jesus Christ was the Son of God
and asked him to come into my heart
when I was 14 years old.
However, I decided to go and do
as I pleased until age 30
when my life seemed no longer worth living.
I had sunk so deep into a lifestyle of sin, depression, and
selfish living that I honestly
could not visualize any way out except death.
To make things worse,
I had a very disturbing dream.
I was inside a hazy tunnel,
I felt the All-Knowing Eyes of The Father
searching me, scanning my soul.
I knew somehow that unless I repented,
judgement/correction might be passed.
I sensed Jesus nearby,
passionately praying for me.
No matter how hard I tried to—
I could not shake this picture from my mind.
Several weeks later I surrendered my life to God.
And through the years I see—

Three great reasons to have HOPE;

The gracious eyes of The Father,
The effectual prayers of The Son,
And the awesome leading of The Holy Spirit!

Our Heavenly Hope
****

God sees our every need,
Jesus intercedes,
and
The Holy Spirit leads!

Jeremiah 24:6-7
"For I will set my eyes upon them for good,
and I will bring them again to this land:
and I will build them, and not pull them down;
and I will plant them, and not pluck them up.
And I will give them an heart
to know me,
that I Am The Lord:
and they shall be my people,
and I will be their God:
for they shall return unto me
with their whole heart." 1

Our Heavenly Hope
****

God will make a way for us!

Isaiah 43:18-20
"Forget the former things; do not dwell on the past.
See, I am doing a new thing!
Now it springs up;
do you not perceive it?
I am making a way in the dessert
and streams in the wasteland....
to give drink to my people,
my chosen,
the people I formed for myself
that they may proclaim my praise." 2

LOOKING FOR HOPE IN ALL THE RIGHT PLACES
(Battle to secure our hope)

This last devotion has a special place
It's purpose is to teach where one's hope
should be placed.
In essence our hope is only safe when
we hope in God!

To hope in God means to place
all our trust in the following:

HIS WORD
Psalms 130:5
*"I wait for the Lord, my soul waits, and in HIS WORD
I put my hope."* 2
John 4:50
*"Jesus replied, You may go. Your son will live. The
man took Jesus at HIS WORD and departed."* 2
1 John 2:5
*"But if anyone obeys HIS WORD, God's Love
is truly made complete in him."* 2

HIS POWER
John 13:3
*"Jesus knew that the Father had put all things
under HIS POWER,..."* 2
Ephesians 3:20
*"Now to him who is able to do immeasurably more
than all we ask or imagine,
according to HIS POWER, that is at work within us,
to him be glory in the church and in Christ Jesus
throughout all generations,..."* 2

HIS MERCY
1 Chronicles 21:13
"David said to Gad, I am in deep distress, let me fall into the hands of the Lord, for HIS MERCY is very great; but do not let me fall into the hands of men." 2
Titus 3:5
"He saved us, not because of righteous things we had done, but because of HIS MERCY." 2

HIS RETURN
Matthew 24:42
"Therefore keep watch, because you do not know on what day YOUR LORD WILL COME." 2
Revelations 22:12
"Behold, I AM COMING soon! My reward is with me, and I will give to everyone according to what he has done." 2

HIS ETERNAL KINGDOM
Matthew 25:34
"Then the King will say to those on his right, Come, you who are blessed by my Father; take your inheritance, THE KINGDOM prepared for you since the creation of the world." 2

HIS PLANS FOR US
Colossians 3:1-4
"Since, then, you have been raised with Christ, set your hearts on things above, where Christ is seated at the right hand of God. Set your mind on things above, not on earthly things. For you died and your life is now hidden with Christ in God. When Christ, who is your life, appears, then you also will appear with him in glory." 2
Sounds like an awesome outcome!!!

SPECIAL THANKS
(Battle partners)

First and foremost I thank the Father, Son, and Holy
Spirit who chose me, saved me, sanctified me
and called me to this work.
You are my hope Lord, so when I give them hope;
I give them God!

My husband is so awesome that I could write a devotional
titled; "Give them Barry!" It was Barry that God spoke to
and said; "Tell Laura to write a book."
Thanks Honey, for all that you've taught me,
but mostly I thank-you for your loyal-love.

To my parents:
Thanks Mom for your prayers, even since your death, I
sense God is still answering your cries in the night.
Thanks Dad for I have received so many of your qualities,
my favorite is determination.

To my Pastor and his precious wife;
Bob and Barbara Miller of Faith Temple, Killeen, Texas:
You have restored my hope through
loving—kindnesses and words that heal.

To my best friend; Ester Magnaye RN
Your devotion to God, family, and imperfect friends make
you a role-model that I'll always respect and admire.

Thanks to Marsha Hoxworth for your encouraging
editorial support and to Daryl Rickard, Colonel,
USAF, Ret. for the cover photo.

128

ENDNOTES

1   Bible. English. King James Version and New Living Translation. 1997. Holy Bible, People's Parallel Edition. Tyndale House Publishers, Inc., Wheaton, Illinois 60189. (a footnote of 1 refers to the New Living translation of this Bible.)

2   The Holy Bible, New International Version. 1983. The Thompson Chain-Reference Bible by the B.B. Kirkbride Bible Company, Inc. (Indianapolis, Indiana 46204) and the Zondervan Corporation (Grand Rapids, Michigan 49506)

**To order additional copies of this book
call toll free: 1 (877) 735-3530**

Volume orders will be discounted.

To share with the author any comments or suggestions
you may contact her via e-mail @
LBlackgtgp@aol.com

Laura is available for radio, television, and church
functions/seminars as the Lord directs.